PRAIRIE STYLE

ARCHITECTURE & DESIGN LIBRARY

PRAIRIE STYLE

Lisa Skolnik

MetroBooks

MetroBooks

©2001 by Michael Friedman Publishing Group, Inc.

ISBN 0-7607-5492-6

Color separations by Colourscan Overseas Co. Pte. Ltd.
Printed in China by C.S. Graphics Shanghai Co., Ltd.

3 5 7 9 10 8 6 4 2

To Howard, whose enduring love of architecture is inspirational and whose unorthodox house-hunting skills situated us in an equally inspiring neighborhood of Prairie-style homes.

Thank you to the talented and diligent staff at Friedman/Fairfax, particularly my editor, Hallie Einhorn. I am grateful for her persistence, diligence, and attention to detail, as well as her vigilant editing to make the text as specific and flawless as possible.

Contents

INTRODUCTION

8

CHAPTER ONE

SITE AND STRUCTURE

16

CHAPTER TWO

LIVING SPACES

40

CHAPTER THREE

PRIME PIECES

60

CHAPTER FOUR

WARM ADORNMENTS

84

INDEX

96

INTRODUCTION

At the end of the nineteenth century, homes across North America sported frameworks and flourishes that paid homage to the structures of ancient Greece and Rome, medieval Europe, seventeenth- and eighteenth-century Spain and France, and the kings and queens of England. Cities, suburbs, and towns were rife with elaborately ornamented homes that embodied a panoply of styles, from frothy Queen Annes sporting turrets, peaks, and wraparound porches to dignified Federal and Colonial Revivals bearing louvered shutters, elegant Ionic columns, and mullioned sash windows.

But as the twentieth century was about to commence, several progressive architects in the Midwest began to design homes that were totally devoid of historical European references. These revolutionary structures were conceived in concert with their environment, namely the flat landscape of the prairie, which eventually lent the style its name. Consequently, these homes sat low to the ground and embraced long, horizontal lines. The horizontal effect was emphasized by broad rooflines, which could be hipped, gabled, or flat but usually had wide overhanging eaves to provide shelter from the sunny and windy environment. These houses were also punctuated by vertical elements, such as soaring casement windows, chimneys, or masonry piers—much like the prairie punctuated by an occasional tree. Conceived as whole entities right down to the fixtures, furniture, and landscaping, which were all given the same importance as the architecture, the homes drew their beauty from their anatomy rather than from applied ornamentation. Inside, they sported simplified, open floor plans composed of fewer but larger rooms that usually radiated from, or related to, a large central living space.

One of the strongest champions of this innovative style was Frank Lloyd Wright, who lived and worked in Chicago around the dawn of the twentieth century. Believing that homes were inflexible, uncomfortable, chaotic, riddled with fussy ornamentation, and entirely unrelated to their surroundings, he sought to redefine residential architecture. Embracing new design principles, he and a group of about twenty other

OPPOSITE: *The 1902 home that Frank Lloyd Wright designed for Ward W. Willits in Highland Park, Illinois, is generally acknowledged to be the first great Prairie residence. Featuring four wings, the structure is based on a cross plan. A close look at the casement windows reveals the linear detailing of the art glass, which was restored by the current owners. Planters and window boxes invite nature to become part of the facade.*

young architects succeeded in doing just that. Eventually, long after the movement had subsided with the advent of World War I, the style that Wright and his peers created came to be called the Prairie School.

In many ways, Wright's thinking echoed the beliefs of Louis Sullivan, his mentor and employer for almost six years. Sullivan, who was the partner of Dankmar Adler in the Chicago firm Adler & Sullivan, had gained fame for his design of the Auditorium Theatre (1886–1890) and the department store Carson Pirie Scott (1899–1904), originally the Schlesinger and Mayer store, as well as for his development of the sky-scraper. He held highly original ideas about design, which he imparted to the young architects of the day. Coining the phrase "form follows function," Sullivan believed a structure should relate to its intended purpose and its site. The buildings inspired by Sullivan's new approach and ideals came to be known as the Chicago School of Architecture.

Although Sullivan was a source of inspiration for the Prairie School architects, he was preoccupied with designing commercial structures. Wright and his peers, however, focused their attention on the home. Wright left Sullivan's firm in 1893, eventually taking an office in Steinway Hall. There, in 1897, he formed a coterie with three other Chicago architects who had offices there: Dwight Perkins, Robert Closson Spencer, and Myron Hunt. All were intent on reinventing the home. Having already achieved success with his first independent com-mission—the Winslow House—which was built in the Chicago suburb of River Forest in 1893, Wright emerged as the leader of the group.

RIGHT: *Banker Arthur Heurtley's dedication to the visual and musical arts encouraged Frank Lloyd Wright to design this elegantly artistic Oak Park, Illinois, home in 1902. A continuous band of casement windows, a hipped roof, and variegated brickwork give the home its long, low-to-the-ground silhouette. Outstretched terraces further contribute to the profoundly horizontal profile while embracing nature.*

ABOVE: *A bay in the living room of Frank Lloyd Wright's Meyer S. May House in Grand Rapids, Michigan, is rimmed with windows and skylights executed in coordinating art glass panels. The configuration floods the room with light and opens the space up to the outdoors.*

In 1898, Wright built a studio next to his home in the Chicago suburb of Oak Park, inviting a group of architects to join him there. As a result, the hub of the Prairie School moved from Steinway Hall to Oak Park. The core group working with Wright included Marion Mahony, John S. Van Bergen, Francis Barry Byrne, William Drummond, and Walter Burley Griffin. Others who subscribed to this philosophy held positions with different firms; George Grant Elmslie and William Steele worked for Sullivan, and George Washington Maher, William Gray Purcell, Thomas E. Tallmadge, and Vernon S. Watson apprenticed under various Chicago architects before striking out on their own. But all of these pioneers had the same goal as Wright, namely to develop a new form of residential architecture that was specifically suited to its environment.

Wright is said to have claimed he sought inspiration from nature, not books or other sources. To him, this meant designing a house to reflect its surrounding landscape and situating it to take advantage of the site, from its terrain to the availability of natural light. Wright also employed architectural devices to bring the occupants of a structure into closer contact with nature whenever possible. This desire to reunite residents with the outdoors was shared by the other proponents of the style, and as a result, Prairie homes usually incorporated a number of porches, terraces, and patios.

While their work was indeed groundbreaking, the Prairie School architects embraced some of the values and design principles promoted by advocates of certain other styles. Perhaps the best known of these is the Arts and Crafts Movement, which was born in England in the late nineteenth century as a protest against Victorian fussiness. At the core of this design philosophy lay a disdain for pretension and a reverence for the honest and forthright use of materials. The Shingle style, which had its genesis in Boston in the 1880s, also had something in common with Prairie architecture, promoting the notion of a relatively open floor plan. The Craftsman style, which looked to the English Arts and Crafts Movement as a guiding force, developed in the western states at the same time the Prairie style was evolving in the Midwest and also demonstrated the belief that each structure should relate to its site and respond to its owner's needs. Meanwhile, the so-called primitive architecture of the American Southwest brought to the forefront the concept of incorporating geometric shapes, arranged in a simplified way. Seen in the larger international context, the Prairie School was primarily a regional manifestation of reform and revolt, similar to the Art Nouveau, Austrian Secession, and Glasgow School movements that had come before it.

To the casual observer, the hallmarks of the Prairie style came to be the use of natural materials, precise forms, continuous horizontals punctuated by short verticals, and the sense that the building belonged to the landscape. But there was one major innovation that was not immediately obvious to the layman, which was the involvement of the architect in every aspect of the home. Like the Arts and Crafts architects of the day, those of the Prairie School strove to design a total environment, which included the furnishings and accessories that were important to the overall aesthetic of the house. Pursuing this goal, the Prairie School architects designed such built-in features as hearths, which served as focal points in living and recreational spaces; sideboards, bookcases, and cabinets for storage; and window seats that served as secluded or completely open perches, depending on the nature of the space in which they were situated. Details were also important. For instance, the motif of the leaded-glass windows in the house was often carried out in the cabinetry and tilework. In short, the Prairie interior was laden with elements that blurred the line between architecture and furniture design.

When they first arrived on the scene, Prairie homes had much to offer their occupants, including to some degree a change in lifestyle. Their flowing, open-plan interiors promoted family togetherness, and the abundance of built-in storage helped to cut down on clutter.

With their promise of simplified living and their beautiful, honest designs, Prairie homes were often featured in the prominent shelter magazines of the day.

The climactic years for the Prairie School came between 1910 and 1916. Not only houses, but public and commercial structures such as banks, offices, churches, libraries, schools, and civic buildings were built in the style as the Prairie School's influence spread throughout the country. Ironically, by that time, Wright had experienced a falling-out with his fellow architects over their success; since the movement eclipsed his work at this point, many others received the prestigious commissions he sought. In 1909, Wright left Oak Park to travel and work in Europe and, later, Japan; ultimately, he moved to Wisconsin, essentially bringing to an end his formal relationship with the Prairie School. Wright heaped scorn on his peers, insisting that the movement had collapsed, but this was far from the case. His departure actually freed the architects he had trained to find their own interpretations of the style.

Despite its popularity, by 1917 the Prairie style was in decline for a number of reasons. The fickle nature of taste was partly to blame, as the public moved on to other trends. But the social changes brought on by the impending war also hastened the decline. When World War I began, a wave of nostalgia and cohesiveness struck the country, and a longing for the sense of tradition and security provided by historical revival styles prevailed. Only after World War II, when public taste again came to favor natural materials and low, small-scale, anti-monumental architecture that related to the earth, did the characteristics of the Prairie house that had been misunderstood the first time around—simplicity, the use of natural materials, open floor plans, and integrated interiors—gain popularity once again. Ultimately, these elements became the basis for the ubiquitous split-level or ranch-style houses of the mid-twentieth century.

For his part, Wright never let go of his ideals, but rather used the same principles he had incorporated in his Prairie-style homes, along with new technological advances, to move forward with his concept of organic architecture. His whole oeuvre of work is, in essence, a stunning example of architecture that is all-American in the truest sense.

The values promoted by the Prairie architects and the refreshing simplicity of their designs are just as applicable and desirable today as they were a century ago when the style debuted. Thanks to their honest beauty, fluid floor plans, and ties to nature, these homes offer a sense of peace and harmony that is greatly sought after. In these pages, we will examine the parameters of the Prairie style and explore its relevance to architecture and interior design today.

OPPOSITE: *Interpretations of Prairie styling continue to find their way into architecture and furniture design today. In this enticing sitting area, two Prairie-style benches and a coffee table complement the sleek geometric motif of the windows. While the view is not one of a prairie landscape, the bands of windows do blur the boundaries between inside and out in pure Prairie style.*

CHAPTER ONE
SITE AND STRUCTURE

Perhaps the most immediately striking aspect of a Prairie home is its powerfully horizontal silhouette. For the most part, this lateral emphasis is achieved by a low, gently sloping roofline with wide overhanging eaves. But the hovering roof is not the only element that plays up the horizontal effect. When the main portion of the home is two or more stories, it is usually flanked by one or two single-story wings that bring the structure back down to earth and create an outward thrust. Geometric forms arranged into rectangular configurations further emphasize the horizontal quality of these homes, as do inset banding trims highlighting such forms. Vertical elements, such as chimneys and piers, tend to be broad and massive, rather than elongated.

A variety of materials was used to build the Prairie house. These buildings could be constructed of wood, plaster (which was tinted off-white and sometimes used in decorative friezes), Roman brick, random-cut limestone, or even concrete. But rarely were more than two building materials combined in a single structure, and the same materials, treated in a similar vein, were used for both the exterior and interior finishes of the home, creating a cohesive environment. For the most part, facades were left unpainted in order to allow the inherent attributes of the materials to shine.

While Wright's influence on the aesthetic of the Prairie School is legendary, many other architects also made significant contributions. For instance, Walter Burley Griffin pioneered the use of concrete and developed a workable system of concrete blocks known as Knitblock, which he patented in 1917, at a time when Wright was just proposing such a concept. (Wright finally employed concrete blocks during the 1920s.) Francis Barry Byrne emphasized severe, space-enclosing cubic shapes for his structures instead of using flowing horizontal shapes punctuated with vertical details; William Drummond accentuated precise geometric forms, making full use of the right angle and the slab roof; William Gray Purcell and George Grant Elmslie, who ultimately

OPPOSITE: *Frank Lloyd Wright's Home and Studio still stands in Oak Park, Illinois. It is here that Wright developed his architectural practice, perfecting the style of the Prairie School. He began construction of the house in the mid-1890s, using $5,000 borrowed from Louis Sullivan; in 1898, he completed the studio annex. As Wright would frequently experiment with new ideas, the structure was in a constant state of renovation and expansion.*

formed a partnership, juxtaposed broad surfaces with sharp-edged voids; and Louis Sullivan, in his post-1900 designs, fused rich, organic ornament with simple, monumental forms.

Given the Prairie philosophy, which also stressed the healthful and spiritual benefits of an outdoor life, the landscape was considered an integral part of the Prairie structure. Terraces and patios were designed to facilitate movement between the home and the grounds, and the house itself often sported ledges and piers topped by built-in planters. The notion of a formal garden was rejected in favor of a natural, even rustic, approach that built on the surrounding terrain, using plants indigenous to, or capable of thriving in, the environment. Yet each Prairie architect approached the garden a bit differently. Frank Lloyd Wright used flowers and trees that grew well in the Midwest and planted them in ways that related to the architecture, while Walter Burley Griffin, who was also trained in landscape design, created gardens that were more ordered and geometric. Chicago landscape architects Jens Jensen and Ossian Cole Simonds embraced a highly organic practice that preserved the natural terrain; employing a progression of plantings, the team created small tableaux that flowed into each other, such as an open meadow leading to an enclosed glen. Today, many homeowners who find the naturalistic quality of Prairie landscaping appealing incorporate gardens that build on the principles developed by the Prairie School.

RIGHT: *A vertical stacking of interlocking rectangular masses and shapes teams up with a much lower, more horizontally oriented wing in Frank Lloyd Wright's William E. Martin House, designed in 1902 and located in Oak Park, Illinois. The interplay of horizontal and vertical components appears again and again in Wright's Prairie designs. In some cases, the juxtaposition is dramatic, as it is here; in other instances, the effect is more subtle.*

LEFT: *Though Louis Sullivan primarily concentrated on tall, commercial buildings, he designed Bradley House in Madison, Wisconsin, as a favor for a cherished client. The 1909 house is the only home by Sullivan to survive today. While the structure soars higher than most other Prairie houses, it has much in common with its counterparts, including deep overhanging eaves, bands of casement windows, and a Roman brick facade. Furthermore, its rooms radiate from the center of the home and lead out to terraces.*

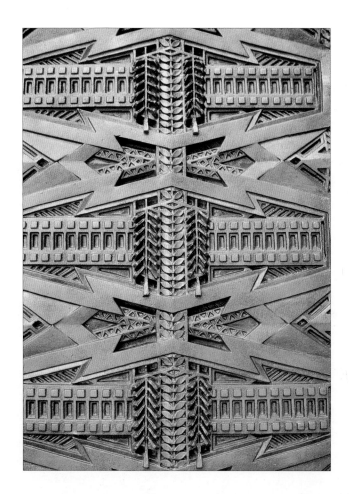

LEFT: *Located in Springfield, Illinois, the Dana-Thomas House was designed by Frank Lloyd Wright in 1902 for Susan Lawrence Dana. At the time that the home was built, it contained the largest collection of site-specific, Wright-designed art glass and white oak furniture, much of which remains intact in the house today. With thirty-five rooms and twelve thousand square feet (1,115 sq m) of living space, the home was designed for entertaining.*

ABOVE: *The ornate terra-cotta tiles on the exterior of the Dana-Thomas House reflect the influence of Louis Sullivan. Though Sullivan designed very few homes himself, he advocated the fusion of rich, organic ornamentation and simple, monumental forms.*

ABOVE: *Walter Burley Griffin's work falls into two categories: the first group reveals Wright's influence, while the second revolves around severe, even abstract forms as well as the creative employment of concrete. Houses in Griffin's later style take the form of closed cubes with few overhanging eaves. The Russell L. Blount House, built in 1912 in Chicago, displays these characteristics.*

ABOVE: *The William N. Clarke House, designed by Walter Burley Griffin in 1913, is part of a grouping of houses that the architect built on the south side of Chicago. In these structures, he pioneered the use of concrete trimmed with wood and experimented with geometric forms. A close look at the silhouette of the house and the configuration of the wood bands reveals an assortment of triangular, rectangular, and pentagonal shapes.*

ABOVE: *Thomas E. Tallmadge and Vernon S. Watson formed a partnership shortly before designing this 1906 home for Lewis H. Lozier in River Forest, Illinois. Replete with the hallmarks of Prairie styling, the house features a sheltered porch that helps to make the outdoors part of residential life. The proximity of the shady tree blurs the distinction between structure and landscape.*

ABOVE: *William Drummond and Louis Guenzel formed a partnership that lasted from 1912 to 1915. Drummond did almost all of the designing while Guenzel attended to business matters. The firm's 1912 Charles J. Barr House, located in Riverside, Illinois, employs several design devices that give it a horizontal emphasis. Thanks to the use of different materials for the first and second stories, the entire facade is split into two rectangular parts. The lower level is accentuated by protruding rows of Roman brick, while the upper level is outlined with bands of wood trim.*

ABOVE: *John S. Van Bergen was the last architect of note to join Wright's studio, which he did in 1909. Fueled by the desire to create what he considered to be "the workingman's cottage," Van Bergen became known for designing elegantly proportioned, smaller homes. This stucco example was built in 1913 for Robert N. Erskine in Oak Park, Illinois.*

OPPOSITE: *The horizontal bearing of Tallmadge & Watson's 1909 Louis A. Tanner House in Chicago is further emphasized by the astute use of wood band trim on the home's facade. By underlining the hipped roof and bands of casement windows, this decorative element visually stresses the width of the structure. A pergola helps to bring nature right up to the doorstep, while the groupings of casement windows seem to dissolve the boundaries between indoors and out.*

ABOVE: *This brick and stucco residence was designed by Frank Lloyd Wright in 1906 for banker Peter A. Beachy. Beachy originally hired Wright to remodel a Gothic cottage that stood on the spot, but the master architect ended up completely rebuilding the house, orienting it at right angles to the street in order to utilize part of the pre-existing foundation. Notice how the entrance—partially obscured by a tree on the front lawn—is located off to the side, a common feature of Prairie houses.*

ABOVE: *The home of Gustavus Babson in Oak Park, Illinois, was designed by the firm of Tallmadge & Watson in 1912. Shown here from the backyard, the house seems solidly grounded, thanks to its striking breadth, low-pitched roof, and overhanging eaves. Window boxes, planters, and a garden of purple blooms keep residents connected to nature.*

ABOVE: *In 1911, Frank Lloyd Wright built a country house and studio for himself in his ancestral stronghold of Spring Green, Wisconsin. The name of the home, Taliesin, comes from the Welsh for "shining brow." A prime example of the integration of structure and site, the home was designed to grow out of the slope and overlook the water below.*

OPPOSITE: *On the side facing away from the lake, the house wraps around an exquisitely landscaped and intimate courtyard that serves as an extension of the interior living space.*

ABOVE: *Robert Closson Spencer, one of the original Prairie School architects at Steinway Hall, favored a somewhat grander interpretation of the style. His more formal slant is evident in McCready House, with its prominent entrance, elegant Roman brick facade, and pronounced hipped roof. Located in Oak Park, Illinois, the house was built in 1907.*

OPPOSITE: *The Prairie School rejected formal European-style gardens in favor of a more natural, unhampered look. Such an approach has been employed in the garden of this period home, which bears many of the marks of Prairie styling.*

OPPOSITE: *While many of the Prairie architects designed art glass to use in the windows and cabinets of their homes, each had his own particular style. Frank Lloyd Wright favored clean, straight lines with geometric patterns because he felt they were most appropriate for modern houses. Art glass doors that recall Wright's work are a fine fit for this contemporary home in Minneapolis.*

RIGHT: *Ornament was an important part of the makeup of a Prairie house. In the movement's earlier years, many designers favored sumptuous embellishment. Later, however, the textures and patterns of the wood and brick used to build the structure were considered to be the primary attraction. This contemporary wood door employs the sort of styling that would be found in more mature examples of Prairie design. Graced by only one sidelight, the doorway also displays the asymmetry typical of many Prairie facades.*

LEFT: *Frank Lloyd Wright experimented with the concepts he espoused, as evidenced by his design for the E.A. Gilmore House, built in Madison, Wisconsin, in 1908. Although the structure has a distinctly horizontal orientation—thanks to the bands of casement windows, the linear arrangement of the wood trim, and the position of the wings—its height contributes a strong vertical element. On account of the home's pronounced jutting eaves, Wright scholars have dubbed the structure the "Airplane House."*

ABOVE: *With its strong horizontals, verticals, and cubic form, as well as its celebration of natural materials, this home, designed in 1987 by the Chicago firm of Quinn & Searl, pays homage to Prairie styling. In keeping with the notion of using indigenous materials, the Lannon stone employed for the house comes from the nearby Fox River Valley.*

CHAPTER TWO

LIVING SPACES

The Prairie house was as revolutionary on the inside as it was on the outside. Gone were the small boxy rooms that enclosed space rather than shaping it and separated family members in the process. Gone was the typical mere smattering of windows that kept nature at bay. And gone were the customary flourishes and frills that had adorned homes of the past.

With its open floor plan, reliance upon natural materials, emphasis on geometric motifs, and integrated design elements, the Prairie home was a study in carefully conceived simplicity. Instead of elaborately milled cornices and frothy fretwork, simple lines and flat planes prevailed.

The traditional arrangement of rooms was replaced by efficient interiors that depended upon head-high partitions, low walls, shifts in ceiling heights and floor levels, and built-in furnishings to define space. The reduction in the number of walls not only allowed air and light to circulate freely, but people as well, thereby facilitating family togetherness. In many Prairie homes, walls were eliminated altogether from the public living areas so as to create smooth, fluid movement; bedrooms and service areas, however, retained their barriers to preserve privacy.

Furthering the open quality of the interior, bands of tall casement windows increased natural illumination, visually expanded the space, and ushered the outdoors into the residence. These stretches of windows were often edged outside by porches, terraces, and balconies, which also extended the boundaries of the interior space past the true physical limits while accentuating the horizontal sweep of the home.

Each member of the Prairie School articulated his or her ideas in a singular manner and handled space and interior ornamentation in a unique way. While Frank Lloyd Wright promoted a horizontal flow, Walter Burley Griffin developed a split-level organization of space. Griffin's wife, Marion Mahony, who designed much of the furniture

OPPOSITE: *The principles that Frank Lloyd Wright advanced are evident in the design of his own Home and Studio in Oak Park. The entry hall flows easily into the area beyond, where a built-in window seat draws the eye and a band of casement windows opens the space up to the outside world. The strategic placement of Oriental rugs accentuates the feeling of fluidity.*

and interior ornamentation for Wright's houses, showed a preference for pinwheel floor plans.

Since the interiors of the Prairie home were executed in the same materials as the exteriors, the Prairie architects used regional woods and brick, employing them in entirely new applications. The use of local woods further linked a home to its environment, uniting the structure with its natural surroundings. Perhaps the most popular wood for living areas was quartersawn oak, which was cherished for its rich graining and durability. Such softer, less expensive woods as birch and pine were employed in the private areas of the home, such as the kitchen and bedrooms. Regardless of the specific type, wood was not usually covered up with paint; instead, it was stained and then waxed to let the texture and grain show through. Just as oak was the wood of choice, narrow gauge Roman bricks were the most coveted type of brick for both outside and indoor use. Inside, these bricks could make up entire walls or simply hearths; either way, their proportions furthered the horizontal aesthetic that the Prairie architect sought to celebrate.

Wright wanted total control over every aspect of his projects and argued against freestanding furniture. He believed everything should be built-in, massive, or inextricably linked to the architectural elements of a place and therefore impossible to remove. George Washington Maher developed an integrated design plan he called the "motif rhythm theory," which took its inspiration from the client's temperament and the local flora; he mined these two elements to develop a guiding motif for each of his homes. These motifs would incorporate both a geometric form and a stylized prairie flower, and would surface in all facets of the home, from the architecture to the furnishings and decorative detailing.

The work of the Prairie architects spawned a stunning array of art glass. Besides gracing the bands of casement and clerestory windows, art glass was used to enhance skylights, built-in cabinets, wall sconces, and lamps. Frank Lloyd Wright and George Grant Elmslie, who were the chief glass designers of the Prairie School, rejected the ornate, opalescent picture windows of Louis Comfort Tiffany and others, and turned to rectilinear designs that echoed the lines of the Prairie home. If privacy was desired, a window would feature more complex designs to eliminate the need for curtains; when a view was preferred, the center of the window was left bare. A large amount of art glass created during the height of the movement remains intact today. But as the style had such a significant impact on the medium, it is also possible to buy a wide variety of exquisite reproductions.

OPPOSITE: *Located on the second floor of George Washington Maher's Magerstadt House, this inglenook encourages residents to soak in the warmth of the Roman brick hearth. A straightforward geometric design graces the end of each built-in seat, counterbalancing the slightly more stylized flower designs that appear in the art glass windows.*

ABOVE, LEFT: *The hidden quality of many Prairie home entrances applies not only to the exterior of the home, but to the interior as well. In Walter Burley Griffin's Rule House, located in Mason City, Iowa, the design of the vestibule keeps it secluded from the rest of the home. Once visitors pass through this area, they enter a more expansive, open space.*

ABOVE, RIGHT: *Wood paneling and posts inlaid with subtle bronze trim are used to transform what was once a plain staircase, bordered by plaster walls and edged with a nondescript railing, into a showpiece of Prairie styling. Rather than being an overt copy of a Prairie pattern, the staircase features a geometric motif that pays homage to the period.*

ABOVE: *As part of an effort to update a Prairie-style home, an "island" of cabinets flanked by built-in shelves is floated in the center of a large living space. The addition is in keeping with the philosophy and aesthetic of the Prairie School, as it manages to serve as a divider without interrupting the flow of space.*

ABOVE, LEFT: *Pursuing their desire to create a unified whole, the Prairie architects incorporated built-in furnishings into their designs. In this home by Tallmadge & Watson, a built-in window seat flows seamlessly out of the surrounding architecture, while the use of art glass for the casement windows makes the perch more inviting.*

ABOVE, RIGHT: *A close-up of one of the art glass windows reveals its delicate geometric pattern. While the lower part of the window features translucent glass for privacy, the upper part remains clear to make the most of the outdoor scenery. Golden tints echo the hue of the prairie.*

RIGHT: *A home doesn't*
necessarily have to be located
on the prairie in order to
have a prairie view. Here,
a pair of Frank Lloyd
Wright windows originally
from the Francis W. Little
House in Peoria, Illinois,
has been installed in another
home and backed with an
oil painting of a prairie
landscape. A Gustav Stickley
fall-front desk and chair,
along with a grille from the
period, round out the tableau.

OPPOSITE: *Frank Lloyd Wright advocated the extensive use of windows to allow a home to relate to its environment and let its residents experience nature in their daily lives. In the Ward W. Willits House in Highland Park, the dining room is rimmed with windows that make the landscape beyond an integral part of the dining experience. The geometric motif in the windows is repeated in the overhead light fixtures, which, executed in creams and golds, cast a warm glow on the dining area.*

RIGHT: *At the far end of the dining room, a light-infused alcove outfitted with built-in seating demonstrates how Wright dictated the way the spaces in his homes should be used. The nook is clearly an enchanting place to sit and commune with nature. Notice how the detailing of the art glass frames the outdoor view.*

ABOVE: *Surrounded by art glass windows, the dining room in Frank Lloyd Wright's 1907 Tomek House invites in plenty of natural light. When the sun goes down, art glass lighting fixtures overhead step in.*

OPPOSITE: *This handsomely executed built-in sideboard is located in the Edward E. Boynton House in Buffalo, New York. The geometric motif that appears in the art glass cabinet doors surfaces again in windows and light fixtures in other parts of the home.*

LEFT: *The butler's pantry in Frank Lloyd Wright's Home and Studio reveals the architect's attention to detail. The configuration of the drawers and the pattern of the panes on the cabinets give the bank of built-in storage a distinctly horizontal orientation.*

BELOW: *This contemporary kitchen has a Prairie demeanor, thanks to the arrangement of the wood band trim. Clerestory windows rim the space and flood the room with light.*

ABOVE: *In a renovation of a turn-of-the-century bungalow, a formerly nondescript stairway receives a dose of Prairie styling. The screenlike configurations of wood recall the grilles used by the Prairie School architects to define space yet maintain openness.*

ABOVE: *The gallery of the Dana-Thomas House is the centerpiece of the wing that was used for entertaining. With its dramatic barrel-vaulted ceiling, emphasized by ribbed arches and edged with site-specific sconces, the space has a lofty appearance. However, the sense of grandeur is counterbalanced by the straightforward materials. The room was originally furnished with print tables designed by Wright to display the owner's collection of watercolors and Japanese prints.*

ABOVE: *In the master bathroom of the Dana-Thomas House, a half-wall sections off the bathtub and toilet. The room is clad in the same lustrous red oak found in the rest of the home. Both the white oak furniture and the red oak paneling and trim used throughout the house were stained a rich mahogany for a unified appearance.*

ABOVE: *The tenets of the Prairie School are still employed today, as evidenced by an inviting contemporary home. The front door sets the tone with its lively, geometric art glass motif surrounded by burnished wood framing.*

RIGHT: *From the central hall of the home, it is evident that the spaces in the residence are not bound by restrictive walls but instead flow into each other. A partition of wooden posts in a linear configuration defines the dining area while permitting the passage of light and air. As a result, both spaces appear larger than they really are.*

ABOVE: *The open, airy main living area of the home from the preceding pages is a testament to the fact that Prairie styling is timeless and well suited to our needs today. The hearth—which, with its articulated horizontal lines, speaks of the Prairie aesthetic—encourages family and friends to gather around, while the abundance of art glass windows suffuses the room with sunlight, making it a pleasant place in which to spend time. A wraparound mural at the far end of the room seems to make the corner dissolve.*

ABOVE: *In true Prairie style, the art glass windows in the bedroom feature the same motif as the front door and the windows in the living area. Reinforcing this sense of continuity, the architecture of the bedroom's hearth echoes that of the fireplace in the living room. Further recalling the work of the Prairie School architects, a Japanese-style mural presides over the hearth.*

CHAPTER THREE
PRIME PIECES

The Prairie School architects held the view that the home should be an integrated whole. Toward that end, they developed a comprehensive and unified style of interior design—which included furnishings of every ilk.

Crafted in wood, these pieces were solidly constructed. They embraced straightforward, rectilinear silhouettes and were relatively unadorned, save for, in some cases, simple geometric flourishes or motifs appearing in the detailing or hardware. Like their built-in counterparts, pieces were stained and waxed in specific ways to highlight the natural grain of the wood. The preferred wood was white oak, fumed to a dark hue with ammonia or given a weathered gray-brown finish; wax was applied in such a way as to impart a quiet, rather than bright, sheen. Pieces tended to be boxy and massive with slablike surfaces, though desks, tables, and cabinets were also made in smaller, delicately proportioned versions. Library tables were particularly popular at the time and varied from hexagonal designs to long, rectangular models that are now used as dining tables. Simple hinges and escutcheon plates of hammered brass, pewter, or copper were used to enhance case pieces, such as cabinets, bookcases, buffets, and desks. Sturdy hard-edged cushions covered in thick linen or burnished leather topped sofas (called settles at the time) and chairs that often featured slat-style frames. Overall, these pieces tended to be solid yet graceful, elegant yet unpretentious.

At the most exclusive levels, the Prairie School architects designed freestanding furnishings as part of their plans for their clients' residences. They would then hire furniture manufacturers to make these pieces. For instance, designer George Mann Niedecken, whose studio was based in Milwaukee, produced Prairie-style furniture from concepts and drawings supplied by Frank Lloyd Wright and other Prairie architects, as well as creating some original designs. Wright is said to have hired at least four different companies to make the tall slat-back chairs he used in the Willits House and the Dana House—one firm in Chicago and three in Milwaukee. He shopped around rather than depending on a single manufacturer because it was of the utmost importance to him that the firm produce the designs on time and within budget. Other Prairie School architects followed Wright's example, and as early as 1902, these studios or companies were also selling their own quite similar designs to the public. Finally, when clients could not afford custom furniture, Wright and other

OPPOSITE: *The rocking chair, which first gained popularity in the nineteenth century, has been translated into many different versions and styles. Here, a Prairie variant of the chair—made by George Mann Niedecken—beckons in Frank Lloyd Wright's Meyer S. May House.*

still exists today, these pieces are extremely expensive. But many of Frank Lloyd Wright's designs are still in production, and numerous sources—ranging from L. & J.G. Stickley, Inc. to individual craftsmen around the country—make attractive, affordable furniture that pays homage to, or emulates, the style.

architects in the movement advised them to buy pieces by New York furniture maker Gustav Stickley, whose designs are commonly classified today as Arts and Crafts.

In fact, Prairie furniture was part of a popular decorating fad that spread all across the United States, and was closely related to, if not inseparable from, the Arts and Crafts, Mission, and Craftsman furnishings made during the same period. Many of the pieces spawned by these movements were so similar in appearance that they were often mixed and matched in Prairie, Craftsman, Mission, and Arts and Crafts homes. The blending of these styles remains a common practice, thanks to their ability to commingle easily.

While a good amount of original furniture by Wright—and a smattering of freestanding furnishings by other Prairie architects—

LEFT: *This suite of furnishings from Stickley's contemporary Mission Collection includes a variety of styles, from the Prairie-style settle and chair to the Morris chair and coordinating footstool in the foreground. The coffee table at the center of the space features the spindled sides often found in Prairie and Mission pieces.*

OPPOSITE: *The Winston House, a Minneapolis residence designed by George Washington Maher, displays an undeniable sense of integrity, thanks to the incorporation of a lamp and dining chair also designed by the architect. Unlike most Prairie dining chairs, which are known for the rigid posture that they elicit, these make a nod toward comfort with their gently curved backs.*

LEFT: *Frank Lloyd Wright's Dana-Thomas House was completely outfitted with furniture and accessories designed by the architect, and most of these pieces still exist today. No detail escaped Wright's attention, as evidenced by a pair of chairs that grace the corners of the balcony over the home's main hall. One is shown here beside a Wright-designed end table. Making a unified statement, both pieces are made of the same beautiful burnished wood.*

OPPOSITE: *Situated underneath the main gallery, which was used for parties, the library in Wright's Dana-Thomas House has a low ceiling. To keep everything in proportion with the ceiling height, Wright designed a squat library table and low-slung seating. He also incorporated a number of built-in bookcases that feature art glass doors to protect the contents.*

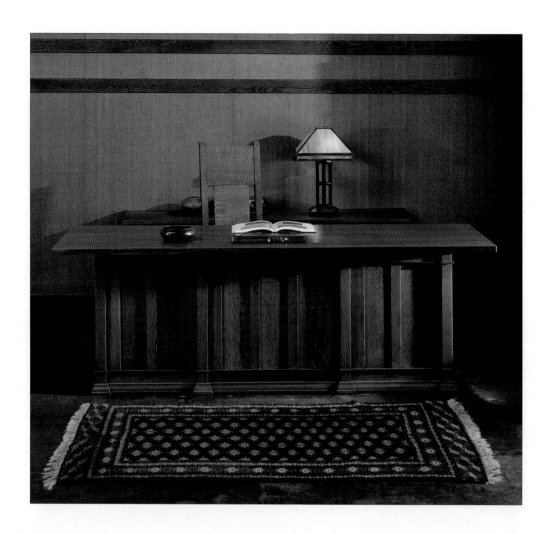

LEFT: *Frank Lloyd Wright designed the furnishings for his Oak Park Home and Studio. In an area intended for reading, a library-style table is surrounded by plank-back chairs. Built-in bookcases and cabinetry provide convenient, out-of-the-way storage.*

ABOVE: *With its articulated piers and planking, a contemporary artisan-made desk combines touches of neoclassical and Prairie styling. However, the overall Prairie aesthetic of the piece is emphasized by its setting. The desk is paired with a chair that is distinctly Prairie in design, as well as a lamp that bears an Arts and Crafts demeanor. Furthermore, the wall features horizontal insets of band trim that evoke the work of the Prairie School architects.*

ABOVE: *All of the original furnishings for Frank Lloyd Wright's Willits House were designed specifically for the residence by the architect and made by local furniture companies. However, during the 1950s, these pieces were sold by the home's second owners at a yard sale. The current owners received permission from the Frank Lloyd Wright Foundation to reproduce pieces from original drawings for the residence. In some cases, Mission and Arts and Crafts furnishings were also used.*

RIGHT: *A Prairie-style armchair, distinguished by its broad, ledgelike armrests, teams up with an Arts and Crafts–style chair for a harmonious effect. The two make an amiable pair, thanks to their flat planes and straightforward lines. The rug, which ties in with the designs featured on the art glass windows, recalls the geometric motifs that Frank Lloyd Wright used during the period.*

OPPOSITE: *Frank Lloyd Wright paid close attention to every detail of the Edward E. Boynton House, right down to requiring that twenty-eight elms be planted on the lot. For the dining room and breakfast area, which flow into each other, he designed furnishings that would work well together. The chairs in both areas match, but the tables are slightly different. The dining table in the main part of the room features wide posts topped by planters and light fixtures for a stately effect. Meanwhile, the table in the breakfast area bears a much simpler profile, sans posts, and reflects the more casual nature of that space.*

ABOVE: *As he did in various other residences, Frank Lloyd Wright designed the dining table of the Meyer S. May House to include built-in lanterns and display niches for plants. Grouping furniture, light fixtures, and nature into a single entity, the composition reflects the architect's goal to achieve a completely unified and seamless environment. Both the table and the built-in cabinetry are made of oak and stained a deep mahogany.*

LEFT: *With its solid posts and art glass lanterns, this contemporary Prairie dining set echoes the designs of Frank Lloyd Wright. The tall-back chairs, with their slablike backs, resemble those of the Meyer S. May House. Together, the chairs and the posts create an enclosure around the table, signifying the importance of family gatherings. The juxtaposition of the table's horizontal lines with the chairs' elongated silhouettes is similar to the balance between horizontals and verticals that pervades Prairie-style architecture.*

ABOVE: *The principles of Prairie styling are also applied to the furnishings in the kitchen of the same home. The slat-back chairs, reminiscent of those designed by Wright, come in two heights to suit the present-day practice of seating diners at a kitchen counter or island. And though freestanding in the center of the kitchen, the wraparound banquette pays homage to the notion of built-in inglenooks championed by the Prairie architects. The ledge along the back recalls those that grace many Prairie-style settles.*

ABOVE: *The interior of a house designed by Tallmadge & Watson illustrates the way in which various types of Arts and Crafts pieces can successfully step in to furnish a Prairie home. The effect is harmonious, thanks to the furnishings' simple, straightforward lines. Plus, both the architectural trim and the furnishings celebrate the natural beauty of wood. In the living room, a Morris-style chair cozies up to the right side of the fireplace.*

ABOVE, LEFT: *In the dining room of the same home, such decorative accessories as a tall case clock, an art glass lamp, and a collection of art pottery accompany the Stickley-style dining set.*

ABOVE, RIGHT: *The same decorating sensibility pervades the bedroom, where an Arts and Crafts–style lantern hangs overhead. As in the more public areas of the home, Oriental rugs are used to define space. Such rugs were a popular choice for floors in period Prairie homes, though many rugs with stylized Arts and Crafts designs were also available.*

ABOVE: *New Stickley furniture is the perfect means for giving a contemporary Prairie-style residence the right ambience and comfort quotient. In this living room, the design of the Prairie-style settle echoes that of the chair across from it, while the linear styling on the sides of both pieces links them to the generously sized coffee table.*

ABOVE: *A similar strategy is applied in the dining room, where contemporary furnishings designed in the period style reign. Thanks to their elegant proportions and geometric lines, these pieces blend in effortlessly with the room's Prairie-style architectural elements, including the massive hearth that not only acts as a space divider but also provides built-in shelving. To form an integrated environment, the wood furnishings have been chosen to match the hue of the wood trim accentuating the fireplace.*

OPPOSITE: *Re-creations of Frank Lloyd Wright designs—including a massive settle and a similarly proportioned table—are perfectly at home in a contemporary residence that pays homage to modernism, the movement spawned by many of the concepts developed by the Prairie School. Thanks to their clean lines and sleek surfaces, the pieces fit right in with the surrounding architecture.*

ABOVE: *Cushions thicker than those that would have been used by Wright in his Prairie period make the settle and armchair much more comfortable than the originals were. The feature on the ledge of the settle echoes a Wright design for a print stand.*

OPPOSITE: *This study features new bookcases designed to look like those of the Prairie era, complete with art glass doors that relate to the motif on the windows in the residence. The easy chairs, ottoman, clock, and lamp all coordinate with the cabinetry, thereby fulfilling the Prairie School demand for a cohesively furnished environment.*

ABOVE: *Carrying out the notion of a unified milieu, the dining room in the same house features a pair of cabinets that match the ones in the study. Prairie styling is evident in the solid, cuffed legs of the table and the tall, spindled backs of the chairs.*

LEFT: *A Prairie-style settle, complete with a distinctively deep frame, holds pride of place opposite the hearth in an inviting living room. Other types of Arts and Crafts furnishings fill the space, imbuing it with coziness and natural warmth.*

ABOVE: *There was no such thing as a Queen-size bed when the Prairie School was popular the first time around. Here, Prairie styling has been applied to a contemporary bed and matching nightstands to create a set that is both handsome and comfortable by today's standards. The Arts and Crafts–style rug enhances the Prairie mood of the room.*

CHAPTER FOUR
WARM ADORNMENTS

The Prairie School's goal to design a total milieu carried through to such details as the decorative objects and the colors used to adorn the walls. But comparatively speaking, the movement was small, and merely a part of the nature-embracing aesthetic that was inspired by the Arts and Crafts Movement popular at the time. While Frank Lloyd Wright realized the kind of fame that allowed him to put his imprimatur on every type of household object, from furniture and textiles to dishes and lamps, no other Prairie architect reached the same pinnacle of achievement. Thus, there are voids in the oeuvre of accessories and adornments that can be attributed to the Prairie School architects and designers. But these were filled more than adequately with objects created by the numerous craftsmen and artisans working in the many styles that today we refer to as Arts and Crafts. In fact, this was a richly varied compendium of styles that had many facets and spun off in many directions. While some designs were far too ornamental for the Prairie home, many were perfectly suited to its straightforward, pared-down demeanor.

Lighting was one of the most obvious elements for the Prairie architects to address. Since many fixtures were built-in, they were legitimately architectural details of the home; plus, the way a space was lit had a major impact on its ambience and functionality. Many of the Prairie architects possessed definite ideas about lighting and designed custom fixtures specific to each project. Often, these fixtures incorporated art glass with geometric motifs that related to the home itself. Frank Lloyd Wright preferred indirect lighting and usually placed the bulbs behind a translucent screen made of rice paper or art glass in a light, creamy hue. The effect was a soft glow, which Wright felt duplicated natural light. The Art Nouveau lamps of Louis Comfort Tiffany were also popular during this period, but the more ornate and colorful examples of his work inspired a reaction in the Prairie architects, who instead used art glass that was stridently simplified. The aesthetic trickled down to the many makers of art glass lamps, resulting in a large supply that was suitable to the Prairie home and also more cost-effective than the designs of Tiffany.

Art pottery was another arena demonstrating wide variations in design, and many versions made by ceramists across the United States

OPPOSITE: *Strong geometric lines and architectural shapes were as pronounced in the decorative accessories used in Prairie homes as they were in the furnishings. These characteristics are obvious in the art glass fixtures, sconces, and Teco pottery that grace this dining room.*

lent themselves perfectly to the Prairie home. One of the most renowned pottery lines was Teco, which came closest to embodying the Prairie aesthetic by merit of its geographic location and the work of its designers. The line, which was first announced in 1899, came from William Gates's American Terra Cotta and Ceramic Company, located in Terra Cotta, Illinois, a small town near Chicago. Gates was a member of the Chicago Architectural Club and president of the Chicago Arts and Crafts Society. He asked fellow group members, including Frank Lloyd Wright and George Grant Elmslie, to design pottery for the Teco line. The company also made architectural and art tiles, as did Pewabic Pottery in Detroit, which is still famed today for the simple Arts and Crafts tiles and pottery it produces. Around the same time, similar work was being created in the Arts and Crafts world by William Grueby, who was one of the most well-known innovators in the field and collaborated widely with Gustav Stickley. Other famed Arts and Crafts pottery companies of the day include Rookwood, Fulper, Newcomb, Roseville, Niloak, and Brush McCoy.

Textiles are the final flourish in any interior, and the Prairie School rejected anything elaborate, romantic, or sweet. Window treatments, tablecloths, upholstery, and pillows were simple, straightforward, and without frills. Made of simple materials, they bore subtle geometric motifs or no patterns at all. Often, tables were left bare or covered merely with runners instead of layers of fabric. Sometimes these runners featured embroidered and appliquéd motifs taken from nature, such as pinecones, thistles, leaves, and dragonflies, and they frequently were arranged in interesting crisscross patterns that permitted the natural grain of the wood table to show. The materials used for table coverings and upholstery were rough-woven, dully finished natural fabrics, such as linen or silk, and they were dyed in such earthy colors as greens, tans, beiges, yellows, or grays. The idea was to use textiles to complement, but never overwhelm, the furnishings.

ABOVE: *Reproduction decorative accessories as well as new pieces that pay homage to the Prairie period are popular today. Shown here are several objects that illustrate this trend. The tabletop lamp has been adapted from a design for a print stand by Frank Lloyd Wright; wood-block landscape prints by a contemporary artist recall those done in the period; and the vase is an exact copy of a Teco design. These items are all joined by an authentic Gustav Stickley spindle bed.*

OPPOSITE: *Frank Lloyd Wright's Frederick C. Robie House, built in 1906, was considered the culmination of the Prairie style thanks to its streamlined, elegant, brown brick and stone facade and its meticulously detailed interior. Even the light fixtures received careful attention; these simple, functional devices seem to flow right out of the wall, thanks to their wooden encasements, which match the architectural trim.*

LEFT, TOP: *Frank Lloyd Wright designed this chandelier for the dining room of the Dana-Thomas House. Five of them are used in the room—one in each corner and another in the center. Today, the design is known as the "butterfly" lamp. The mural in the background was done by George Mann Niedecken, an interior architect who also often oversaw the production of furniture for various Prairie architects.*

LEFT, BOTTOM: *Frank Lloyd Wright, along with the other Prairie architects, would create site-specific art glass motifs based on a geometric element from the house or an abstract portrayal of a prairie plant. In the art glass of the Dana-Thomas House, the prairie sumac became an interlocking pattern of green and gold chevrons and rectangles. Shown here is one of the 168 identical sconces he used throughout the house.*

ABOVE: *Because the Dana-Thomas House was built for entertaining, Wright placed a great deal of emphasis on the home's entry.*
A majestic arched door leads into a dramatic foyer, which features a sculpture by Arts and Crafts artist Richard Bock.

OPPOSITE: *George Washington Maher developed the "motif rhythm theory," in which all the decorative details of a home would be drawn from a specific prairie plant and geometric shape. These two elements would be combined in art glass windows, murals, and mosaic tile fireplace surrounds such as the one shown here. Although the tiles—designed by George Washington Maher and Louis Millet—no longer grace their original residence, they make a harmonious addition to their new home.*

ABOVE, LEFT: *Glass mosaic murals were often placed above and around Prairie fireplaces to help transform the hearth into the focal point of the room. The tiles shown here were designed by George Washington Maher.*

ABOVE, RIGHT: *Thanks to its combination of flat planes and glowing orbs, this light fixture with art glass detailing is perfectly at home in a Prairie residence designed by Guenzel & Drummond.*

OPPOSITE: *With their earthy matte green finish and forms that pay homage to nature, pieces of Teco pottery relate easily to the Prairie School's philosophy. Their shapely curved silhouettes also soften the sharp geometric lines of the furnishings used in these homes.*

RIGHT: *The organic shapes of Teco vases look just as singular and eye-catching in a sleek contemporary setting as they do in Prairie-style homes.*

OPPOSITE: *Frank Lloyd Wright considered virtually every detail in the homes he designed, right down to the linens. He preferred long runners, such as those shown here on a dining table in the Dana-Thomas House. By leaving parts of the table uncovered, the architect allowed the beautiful luster of the wood grain to remain on view. Plus, the runners could be rearranged constantly in various patterns. The ones pictured here are edged with a geometric pattern in a soft golden hue that echoes the tint of the art glass windows.*

ABOVE: *Linen table dressings in the style favored by the Prairie architects are still made and used today. Like the originals, they often sport botanical patterns, such as floral or leafy motifs. The designs are stylized representations rather than realistic depictions.*

INDEX

Accessories, 84–95
"Airplane House," *38, 39*
Arches, 54, *54*
Art glass, 12, *12*, 23, *36*, 37, 42, 46, *46*, 50, *50*, *51*, 68, *69*, 75, *75*, 88, *88*
Arts and Crafts style, 13, 62, 67, *67*, 68, *69*, 74, *74*, 75, *75*, *82*, 83, 85, 86

Babson House (Gustavus), 31, *31*
Balconies, 41
Barr House (Charles J.), 27, *27*
Bathrooms, 54, *55*
Beachy House (Peter A.), 30, *30*
Bedrooms, 59, *59*, 75, *75*, 83, *83*
Benches, 14, *15*
Blount House (Russell L.), 24, *24*
Bock, Richard, 88
Bookcases, 13
Boynton House (Edward E.), 50, *51*, *70*, 71
Bradley House, *20*, 21
Brick, Roman, 10, *11*, 17, *20*, 21, 27, *27*, 34, *34*, 42
Byrne, Francis Barry, 13, 17

Cabinets, 13
Ceilings
    barrel-vaulted, 54, *54*
    low, 64, *65*
Chairs
    Arts and Crafts, 68, *69*
    dining, 62, *63*, *72*, 73
    easy, *80*, 81
    Morris, 62, *62*, 74, *74*
    plank-back, *66*, 67
    rocking, *60*, 61
    slat-back, 61
    tall-back, *72*, 73
Chicago School of Architecture, 10
Chimneys, 9, 17
Clarke House (William N.), 25, *25*
Craftsman style, 13, 62

Dana-Thomas House, *22*, 23, 54, *54*, *55*, 61, 64, *64*, *65*, 88, *88*, *89*
Desks, 67, *67*

Dining rooms, *48*, 49, *49*, 50, *50*, 56, *57*, *70*, 71, *72*, 73, 75, *75*, 77, *77*, 81, *81*, *84*, 85
Doors
    arched, 88, *89*
    art glass, *36*, 37, 56, *56*, 64, *65*, *80*, 81
    contemporary, 37, *37*
    sidelights, 37, *37*
Drummond, William, 13, 17, 27

Eaves, 9, *20*, 21, 24, *24*, 31, *31*
Elmslie, George Grant, 13, 17, 42, 86
Entrances, 34, *34*, 40, 41, 44, *44*, 88, *89*
    side, 30, *30*
Erskine House (Robert N.), 28, *28*

Floor plans
    open, 9, 13, 41
    pinwheel, 42
Furnishings, 23, 60–83
    built-in, 13, 41, 42, *43*, 46, *46*, 49, *49*, 50, *51*, 52, *52*, *66*, 67, 71, *71*
    Stickley, 47, *47*, 62, *62*, 75, *75*, 76, *76*

Gardens, 18, 31, *31*, 34, *35*
Gilmore House (E.A.), *38, 39*
Griffin, Walter Burley, 13, 17, 18, 24, 25, 41, 44
Guenzel, Louis, 27

Hearths, 13, 42, *43*, 58, *58*, *59*, 59, 74, *74*, 77, *77*, *82*, 83
Heurtley House (Arthur), 10, *11*
Hunt, Myron, 10

Inglenooks, 73, *73*

Jensen, Jens, 18

Kitchens, 53, *53*, 73, *73*
Knitblock, 17

Lamps, 42, 62, *63*, 67, *67*, *80*, 81, 86, *86*
    art glass, 50, *50*, *72*, 73, 75, *75*, 85
Art Nouveau, 85

Arts and Crafts, 75, *75*
    "butterfly," 88, *88*
    hanging, 88, *88*
    overhead, *48*, 49
Landscape, 18
Linens, *94*, 95, *95*
Little House (Francis W.), 47, *47*
Living rooms, 58, *58*, *82*, 83
Lozier House (Lewis H.), 26, *26*

Magerstadt House, 42, *43*
Maher, George Washington, 13, 42, 62
Mahony, Marion , 13, 41
Martin House (William E.), 18, *19*
May House (Meyer S.), 12, *12*, *60*, 61, 71, *71*
McCready House, 34, *34*
Mission style, 62
Motif rhythm theory, 42
Murals, 58, *58*, 59, *59*

Niedecken, George Mann, 61, 88

Patios, 13, 18
Pergolas, 28, *29*
Perkins, Dwight, 10
Piers, 9, 17, 18, 67, *67*
Planters, *8*, 9, 18, 31, *31*, *70*, 71
Porches, 13, 26, *26*, 41
Pottery, 75, *75*, 85
    Arts and Crafts, 86
    Pewabic, 86
    Teco, *84*, 85, 86, *92*, *93*, *93*
Purcell, William Gray, 13, 17

Robie House (Frederick C.), 86, *87*
Roofs, 17
    flat, 9
    gabled, 9
    hipped, 9, 10, *11*, 28, *29*, 34, *34*
    low-pitched, 31, *31*
    slab, 17
Rugs, 40, 41, 68, *69*, 75, *75*
Rule House, 44, *44*

Sconces, 42, 54, *54*, *84*, 85
Settles, 61, 62, *62*, 73, *73*, 76, *76*, *78*, 79, *79*, *82*, 83
Shingle style, 13

Sideboards, 13
Simonds, Ossian Cole, 18
Skylights, 12, *12*, 42, 49, *49*
Spencer, Robert Closson, 10, 34
Stairways, 53, *53*
Steele, William, 13
Stickley, Gustav, 47, 62, 86
Sullivan, Louis, 10, 13, 17, 18, 21

Tables, *78*, 79
    coffee, 14, *15*, 62, *62*, 76, *76*
    dining, *70*, 71, *72*, 73
    end, 64, *64*
    library, 61, 64, *65*, *66*, 67
Taliesin, 32, *32*, *33*
Tallmadge, Thomas E., 13, 26, 28, 31, 46, 74
Tanner House (Louis A.), 28, *29*
Terraces, 10, *11*, 13, 18, *20*, 21, 41
Textiles, 86
Tiffany, Louis Comfort, 42, 85
Tomek House, 50, *50*

Van Bergen, John S., 13, 28

Watson, Vernon S., 13, 26, 28, 31, 46, 74
Willits House (Ward W.), *8*, 9, *48*, 49, 61, 68, *68*
Window boxes, *8*, 9, 31, *31*
Windows, 49
    art glass, 12, *12*, 42, *43*, 46, *46*, 50, *50*, 58, *58*, 59, *59*, 68, *69*
    casement, *8*, 9, 10, *11*, *20*, 21, 28, *29*, *38*, 39, *40*, 41, 42, 46, *46*
    clerestory, 42, 53, *53*
    geometric motif in, 14, *15*
    leaded, 13
Window seats, 13, 46, *46*
Wings, 17, *38, 39*
Winslow House, 10
Winston House, 62, *63*
Wright, Frank Lloyd, 9, 10, 13, 14, 30, 32, 37, 39, 41, 42, 49, 50, 61, 64, 67, 71, 85, 86, 95
Wright Home and Studio (Frank Lloyd), *16*, 17, 52, *52*

PHOTO CREDITS

©Philip Beaurline: pp. 7, 56 left, 56–57, 58, 59, 72–73, 73 right

©Mary L. Beck: pp. 68–69

©Judith Bromley: pp. 43, 63, 86, 95

Courtesy of Douglass Hoerr Landscape Architecture: ©Linda Oyama Bryan: p. 35

©Rob Gray: pp. 2, 78, 79, 82–83, 84, 90, 92

Courtesy of Hedrich Blessing: © Jon Miller: pp. 16, 40, 52, 66–67

©Thomas A. Heinz: pp. 32, 44 left, 50, 91 left, 91 right

©Warren Hile Studio: p. 67 right

Courtesy of Katherin Quinn Architects: ©Steve Hall/ Hedrich Blessing: pp. 39 right, 44 right

©Bruce Leighty: p. 34

©Paul T. McMahon: pp. 20–21, 38–39

Courtesy of Michael FitzSimmons Decorative Arts: p. 47

©Robert Perron: p. 70

Photofields: ©Tony Berardi: pp. 5, 8, 23 right, 45 (Architect: Eric Mullendore), 46 left, 46 right, 48, 49, 53 left, 54, 55, 64, 65, 68 left, 74, 75 left, 75 right, 88 top, 88 bottom, 89, 93 (Architect: Lonn Frye)

Courtesy of Pinecrest, Minneapolis, MN: pp. 36, 37

©Paul Rocheleau: pp. 12, 51, 60, 71, 87, 94

©James P. Rowan: pp. 10–11, 18–19, 22–23, 24, 25, 26, 27, 28, 29, 30, 31

©David Schilling: pp. 53 right, 76, 77

©Kay Shaw: p. 33

Courtesy of Stickley: p. 62

Courtesy of Swartzendruber Hardwood Creations, Goshen, Indiana www.swartzendruber. com: pp. 15, 80, 81, 83 right